My name is Asif Ali. I a. ...rite
Art Touches Life, being ...e found my
about matters which mak
identity in poetry. Poetry . I have been writing
poetry for some twenty yea. ....ng a diverse array of topics
and subjects. My poems touch everyone – young, old and in between.

My poetry is a very small or tiny segment of my writing. The other form of writing I pursue is essays. Whatever the genre, I look most of all for depth and weight in the subject. I try as best as I can to understand the subject and then bring forth what I learn in my writing, whether it is poetry, essay or speech. I love music and songs. I need songs and music to inspire and move me in every way. I seek the depth and meaning of songs, and the singer's performance and delivery of the song. Certain singers I admire are **Eva Cassidy**, **Carole King** and **Shakira**. Each are unique and talented for their understanding and application of the music they compose and perform. Though Eva Cassidy mainly sang covers, her voice and insight are so unique. Other languages have their own unique facets and musical personalities. Song and music are essentially for the heart and spirit. As a poet, I look at lyrics very closely. I have been praised for my poems by the musicians I have met who have suggested collaborations.

Dear Lora

I trust you are well. All this time, I have not known your name. I hope you shall find sufficient themes of interest in this book. I write all the time. I am Aquarian and Aquarians are highly creative and original (Shakira is Aquarian).
All the best

Asf.

I dedicate this book to my family, friends and God, without all of whom I would not have written this book. To my special friends.

Asif Ali

CHAT UP RHYMES

AUSTIN MACAULEY PUBLISHERS™
LONDON • CAMBRIDGE • NEW YORK • SHARJAH

Copyright © Asif Ali (2019)

The right of Asif Ali to be identified as author of this work has been asserted by him in accordance with section 77 and 78 of the Copyright, Designs and Patents Act 1988.

All rights reserved. No part of this publication may be reproduced, stored in a retrieval system, or transmitted in any form or by any means, electronic, mechanical, photocopying, recording, or otherwise, without the prior permission of the publishers.

Any person who commits any unauthorised act in relation to this publication may be liable to criminal prosecution and civil claims for damages.

A CIP catalogue record for this title is available from the British Library.

ISBN 9781528903790 (Paperback)
ISBN 9781528903899 (Kindle e-Book)
ISBN 9781528957540 (ePub e-Book)

www.austinmacauley.com

First Published (2019)
Austin Macauley Publishers Ltd
25 Canada Square
Canary Wharf
London
E14 5LQ

I acknowledge all my friends, family and Austin Macauley Publishers for believing in me and my work.

Table of Contents

Preface	11
Foreword	12
'Our Dreams'	18
As We Look Around for Our Spent Youth	19
3 (A) If You're Disabled, You Have Already Been Labelled	20
3 (B)	22
A Start of Us – A Part of Us	23
Greatest Test is Finding Our Best	24
Every Thing and Every One Passes	25
Dickens, the Great Social Writer	26
Death Opens the Door	27
Each One Has to Make a Sacrifice	28
Beauty	30
Art Brings a Sublime Beauty to Tragedy	31
How Are You Feeling?	32
Love Marriage	33
Re-united	34
Life Is the Object of Our Desires	35
All the Nameless Faces	36
Poet's Eyes – Poet's Guise	37
Traditions	38
Being Alone Is Safety in Isolation	39
Sweet and Sour Dreams	41

Uncertainty Is Our Only Certainty	*42*
The Humble Speak the Universal Language	*43*
Limitations and Potentials	*44*
Can We Exist Without Technology?	*45*
The Connection Between Our Brain and Mouth	*46*
Love is a Wonderful Feeling	*47*
Plus and Minus	*48*
Words and Music	*49*
What Is Important?	*50*
Prevalence of the Materialistic	*51*
Knowledge	*52*
Damage or Injury is Not Always Visible	*53*
Being Human Is More Than a Genetic Reality	*54*
The Brain's Vast Information Storage	*55*
Machines Should Never Be Considered in the Absolute	*56*
Like a Good Book, Life Comes to an End	*58*
Public Face – Private Make-Up	*59*
The World Will Always Overwhelm Us	*60*
What Does It Mean to Be a Human Being?	*61*
What Does It Mean to Be a Human Being? (2)	*63*
A Wise Counsel	*65*
Life Breeds Life	*66*
Everyone Wants to Change Something	*67*
Human Spirit	*68*
Life's Unique Language	*69*
An Electronic Universe in a Social World	*71*

Preface

Hello dear reader,

You may or may not be familiar with my previous and debut work of poetry, *When Art Touches Life*. If you have read or are familiar with the book, you will know of my poems. My debut published in 2009, from an artistic perspective, has been well received. From a creative perspective, I am very satisfied.

I chose the title *Chat-Up Rhymes* as the poems may enable readers something of universal interest and similarity about which to converse. Sometimes we think or feel we have nothing of interest and similarity to share with others. Poems and art in general offer viewers a common platform of interests.

If my new work, *Chat-Up Rhymes*, can make people come together through conversation and communication, I will be very pleased. Rhyme does what music and art do, in that it draws people of diverse and differing backgrounds to one point. From personal experience, via poetry I have found I can chat or converse with great ease. All it takes is one audible voice for there to be a conversation amongst many.

The title of this book came out on the day I composed a poem titled 'Human Dart'. I feel the title *Chat-Up Rhymes* is catchy and snappy, makes its point and should get people's instant attention. In such a noisy world, there are millions of silent voices, too silent to be heard. The voice of the silent is permanent. In all hope, this book will be a platform for all the silent voices, mine amongst many. I have always been an introvert. This book will be my voice piece.

Foreword

Since my debut book, *When Art Touches Life*, was published in 2009, I have been very busy. Since the time my book was published, much has changed, much has stayed the same, but regardless, I have carried on writing poetry and essays. I love to write, I find something unique and distinct in my poetry. I write, on average, three poems a day. Artistically, my debut has been successful, far exceeding my expectations.

I hope my new book, *Chat-Up Rhymes*, satisfies the readers as much as my debut. I have made many friends through my poetry. Knowing my poems are enjoyed does much to please my heart. I hope my poetry has universal benefit and meaning.

Don't Brand Me

Anyone who tries to brand me
Does not really understand me.

The Brain's Not So Smart

The brain is not so smart
It does not understand the heart.

Loss of Touch

Nothing hurts as much
As the loss of touch.

Human Kindness

It is said that sharks remain afloat
While the rest sink without trace
In a world which is so cut-throat
Kindness will never drop out of the human race.

The Passing of Summer

With the passing of summer
Many a soul grieves
With a lot fewer sun-kissed hours
In the midst of our footsteps, we
brush the leaves
Dropped down by wintry showers.

Love Gentler Than the Softest Petal

Is stronger than the hardest
Metal.

A Human Dart

If love is a dart
Its aim is the heart.

Tear Today – Gone Tomorrow?

Which sights and sounds known to science
Which of these known to our eyes and ears
Can ever reach our farthest silence
And vanquish all our private tears?

Mind and Heart

If you're smart
You'll touch the mind
You'll touch the heart
If you're kind.

Time

Time we have, it fills me
With sorrow
Time we have, it makes me weep
Time we have, I don't want
To borrow
Time we have, I want to keep.

To See Loved Ones Part

To see loved ones part
It breaks love's heart.

The Food of Love

One intake of food is never enough
Without more, we will die of hunger
One intake of love is more than enough
To make us feel years younger
Whereas food is vital and supplemental
It lasts only so long
Love is food for the heart, making us
Feel alive and strong.

With Each Passing Second

With each passing second of our breath
The clock ticks quicker to our death.

Still Friends?

For us to stay friends, I make no demands
Whether we stay friends, I leave in your hands.

Mementoes of Life

Old age is a fading reflection of one's former self
All one has to show are mementoes on one's shelf.

'Our Dreams'

We perceive reality with our being
We think we know what we are seeing
But are our perceptions not a disguise
For what truth we don't have the eyes
In our dreams, we see other sides
To which in our day's reality hides
We try to unravel the mysteries our dreams hold
But they are like carpets which are not rolled
Dreams hold our every dream and fear
Which become real the moment we can see and hear
Like Sigmund Freud, we can try to unravel
A journey we must all travel.

As We Look Around for Our Spent Youth

We are young one day, yet old another
By which time, our family may consist only of a sister and brother
Whatever we feel and think in youth, time defeats us in old age
With life's book almost over, we may be on our last page
We had our plans and hopes in our younger days
As we moved and grooved in so many different ways
We might look around in search of our long-lost friends
As we hold on in desperation and feint hope before life ends
Pride and energy are what we have aplenty in youth
In old age do we finally accept the terminal truth.

3 (A)
If You're Disabled, You Have Already Been Labelled

Whomever we may be and wherever we go
If we are able-bodied, people's help will be none too slow
If we are a healthy and vital part of the community
We will be welcomed at this and that party.

Lo and behold, if you are lame or disabled
By those in positions of authority, you have already been labelled
To your chagrin, you may not be treated as an equal
You will be lucky if you get as much as a role in a sequel.

People have their minds conveniently preconditioned and set
It matters little to them that you they have never met
They think that you they have figured and understood
They are happy as long as you do not lift your hood.

By many, the disabled are not treated as another human being
The able-bodies allow their prejudices cloud what they are seeing
Life for you will be tough enough if you have a deformity
Or some form of visible and perceptible abnormality.

But the real disabled are all the heartless fools
Who are happy to blindly accept all the silly social rules
They are happy as long as their security is not jeopardised
And their property and possessions are, from them, not prized.
The disabled are constantly belittled, told they have no soul

The disabled are portrayed as being incomplete, not whole
Some of the able-bodied do not seek parity with the disabled
Their only notion of you is that you are by someone labelled.

As long as you are in some eyes seen as sick
To them, you will continue to remain a statistic
They do not like statistics, unduly responding
As far as they are concerned, with you they will not be bonding.

The reason people do not accept the disabled is prejudice
These very people make so much fuss over injustice
When their very security comes under threat
Do they realise there is no such thing as a safety net?

The disabled are never allowed to feel secure in a world with no heart
Where, in spite of their talents and gifts, they are offered a token part
They simply become another face we let slip away
Who we reluctantly allow into our offices and homes to work and play.

3 (B)

Only when we stop looking at the disabled as objects on a shelf
Will we remove the ignorance and bigotry, embedded within our self
When the day comes the disabled are incorporated into society as a whole
Will we return their integrity, self-esteem and soul.

Contrary to popular myth, a disability is not a disease but a freak event
In which they will make what they can of life, in the time they are lent
Another popular myth which should be destroyed is that the disabled are less able
For humanity's sake, please, let's peel off this out-of-date and misplaced label.

A Start of Us – A Part of Us

We are all a product of birth
To venture forth on sections of earth
We will live and we will die
We will laugh and we will cry.

We all have a start of us
Whether we know, the soul is a part of us
Life has yet to be understood
So many tried, thinking that they could.

We all began life as a baby
Happy and sad – there is no maybe
We all have our roads to explore and travel
We all have our puzzles and mysteries to unravel.

What is an intrinsic and integral part of us
Is an element we have had since the start of us
What we become later and what we feel
Is a part of the cards life to us does deal.

Greatest Test is Finding Our Best

We have so little time on earth
When will death come after birth?
It might come soon, it might come late
It makes no difference to our ultimate fate.

Death comes to all then and now
When we think of our mortality do we so bow
Until behind the curtain, death does hide
In our ignorance and folly, we are so full of pride.

When we come close to the ultimate life test
Do we look within and bring out our best?
Until that moment arrives, we continue with our ways
Confident we can do what we want in our remaining days.

We have so many talents which remain latent
Only the creative and spiritually alive find a patent
The rest allow their talents go to waste
Never allowing others to have a taste.

Some leave their best concealed inside a box
Never removing the chains and locks
When we do not bring out our best from inside
All that stops us is our folly and pride.

Every Thing and Every One Passes

Life is a journey we all travel
A mystery that time does unravel
What happened today may happen tomorrow
We discover in this short life, we all borrow.

Everything and everyone does gradually pass
As time and events do naturally amass
We were on a ride, venturing to times anew
Before the final breaths we all drew.

Our future may be unknown and a mystery
One day, to become a chapter in our history
We will be happy and we will be sad
We will be despondent and we will be glad.

Like the wind, everything in life will pass
Like water that was once full in a glass
When life and the future seemed so permanent
We thought little of time that came and went.

Dickens, the Great Social Writer

There are people who come and go
Who help us to develop and grow
They are great for sure
By changing my life and your
One man harboured pain in his life
Living with his indescribable sadness and strife
Charles Dickens was an abandoned child
Who sorely missed being happy and wild
'Tis our good fortune, he wrote his books
In which he showed many notorious crooks
But he also showed us humanity's better side
Some people do hide
If we had never read *Oliver Twist*
We would know not what a gem we might have missed
None of Dickens characters was ever a stooge
We need only see our meanness in Mr Scrooge
One who longed for something he had missed
Mirrored his life in his like-named Oliver Twist.

Death Opens the Door

In life, we go this and that way
Day follows night and night follows day
We will achieve so much as we go on
What will the culmination of our lives be the day we are gone?
While alive, we wonder what lies behind death's door
What is life like when we are no more
When death beckons, the door is opened for always
Then we realise that on Earth, no one stays
Perhaps then we will never again need to think of Planet Earth
On which we were accorded the privilege of living as a result of our birth.

Each One Has to Make a Sacrifice

We are all part of this thing called life
Today, you might find happiness, tomorrow strife
One day, your life will be set on a station on your dial
But whatever happens, never lose that beautiful smile.

No one has things quite his or her way
You might wake up one person but be different at the end of the day
No one really knows what awaits them at any moment
We have no real claim on time, only what we are sent.

Each one has to make some sacrifice
To some, it will mean little; to others, a very heavy price
At some stage, we all lose some of what we once had
Some will control their feelings, others will simply go mad.

Life is never meant to be a piece of cake
Some days, it will for us be a medium; yet others, a burnt steak
However life turns out for you, keep your hopes high
The longer you can, the less chance you will break down and cry.

To sacrifice simply means to relinquish
Instead of having it all, you have less on your dish
All of us would love a full and whole life
What dish you have may be more when you cut with a knife.

Use what you have today and tomorrow

Life and time are ours simply to borrow
We all lose something or other in our days
Life with or without a sacrifice is really a transitional phase.

Beauty

Beauty resides on the face and in the heart
With the passing of time, not getting dull or tired
From the source of life, beauty never drifts apart
As beauty, the Creator of life has made inspired.

In our early days, of beauty we have no recognition
This we go to great lengths to deny
Of the above, we find that ignorance is our admission
If we only seek beauty for the eye.

Beauty resides in the heart and on the face
Though we may judge beauty according to the latter
When beauty is something we can embrace
We will accept that outer beauty does not matter.

True beauty is something many seek but do not find
If beauty is something so elusive and apart
If it is something that is a state of mind
But not the state of the human heart.

Art Brings a Sublime Beauty to Tragedy

People come and people go
Some prefer anonymity, while others a big show
Television has opened the floodgates for you and me
It has become simpler for the camera to record what we see
An artist, unlike gadgets, can look inside the heart
And tell emotional fiction and fact apart
Art attempts at bringing beauty to human tragedy
Words, paintings and music can paint a picture about you and me
Paintings and words are more potent than a camera
In bringing us a wider and deeper panorama
Our electronic gadgets do not reveal what we feel
As they focus on the visible, but what resides on the inside, they conceal
Good art can locate hidden joy and sadness
And in so doing, try to make some sense of our madness
All great books and paintings will forever fascinate the human being
As great artists will feed appreciative eyes something worth seeing.

How Are You Feeling?

We all have to make something of this life
We have our share of happiness and strife.
Some days, we might be on top of the world
Some days, upon us will vitriol and abuse be hurled.

How are you feeling today?
How many sweets has life placed in your tray?
I hope if in the mud you are stuck
Glad tidings come along and change your luck.

Feelings and thoughts so rapidly change
Life, as we discover, comprises a huge range
Never allow yourself a single negative feeling
You never know what cards tomorrow's life will be dealing.

Love Marriage

Love is the marriage of human lives
How many in love are husbands and wives?

Re-united

If it is true that parting is such sweet sorrow

Then our reunion will make me happy tomorrow

Until we meet, you will brighten my every hour

As of sunshine, your memory is the solar power.

Life Is the Object of Our Desires

Being defined by time, we are designed to be
Being confined by life, we are resigned to be
Life is an ongoing time of mysteries
Time is an ongoing life of histories.

What happened in the past, each present is sure to follow
What seeds previous lives have sown, the future is sure to swallow
Time in life will naturally teach us much
The former and latter will touch.

What time make us, others will eventually find
When death has taken us, legacies we leave behind
Time for life is something we embrace
We unconsciously use at our own pace.

All the Nameless Faces

Hello there, fellow traveller, what is your name?
I want to place your face inside a picture frame
We see all those nameless faces
Shying away from warm embraces.

The name is our second intro to a stranger
Does the name allay every sense of danger?
If people simply pass us unnoticed today
We will all carry on our separate ways.

How some tragedy and misery unite the nameless faces
Through dripping tears of sadness, everyone embraces
When the height of the tragedy dies down
All the nameless faces pack up and leave town.

Poet's Eyes – Poet's Guise

When people see me in my poet's guise
I see them through a poet's eyes.

Traditions

We are constantly waging a battle or war with changes. What prevails is very hard to say. The traditions of and in life are very important to many maintaining and upholding our ways of life. Sooner or later, most worldly structures and customs crumble and break down.

Traditions, which include families, history, senses of identity, customs, manner, etc., keep societies bonded as one unit. When changes occur, and they will, there are bound to be differences and rifts of opinion. Change is rarely desirable, we accept it, albeit reluctantly, as a fact of life. We may accept general changes as long as they only remotely affect us. Our changes are not always conducive to our well-being, some changes are forced upon us.

If we have some traditions which to refer to even in times of great change, we will have some stability. Those who relinquish or lose their traditions may find it immensely difficult coping with change.

Being Alone Is Safety in Isolation

We do what we have to. We are all social beings in need of all the ingredients which go towards giving us that certain humanitarian feeling. We feel for others when they are bereaved. We feel for others when they are celebrating. What we see in others, we recognise in ourselves deep down, we are no different.

They are those who live in isolation, laughing at their own jokes, crying when they hurt, yet perfectly happy to continue in this guise. There may be any number of reasons why certain people feel more comfortable in their own company, rather than wishing to indulge in hours of social companionship. The extroverts can adapt into any environment. To speak of natural adjustments is one thing, but in practice, we find it rather more difficult.

Some people prefer being alone, as it gives them a sense of well-being. The lonely probably feel most at home, indulging in contemplative pursuits, e.g., painting, writing, reading, taking walks, inventing, travelling, etc.

Loneliness is safety in isolation. Socializing is safety in numbers. Loneliness is a state of isolation and refuge from the outside world. There may be any number of reasons why this style of life appeals more than one spent in the company of friends. Each one of us seeks refuge in something. We seek refuge in friends, food, travel, books, etc.

Some seek refuge in their own isolation. For some, isolation is a great comfort, as it enables for the nastier and horrific elements in the world to be removed or shut out.

For some, isolation offers this sense of security. We all know that we cannot bury our heads in the sand and never see what is happening above the parapet.

All refuges are temporary affairs. We try to cling on to the refuge which makes us feel safest. Yet deep down, we know that this sense of safety will one day be shattered, and we will have to integrate into the wide world.

For the lonely, the world is a television screen, with the barrier between them and us. When we come across a scene or picture we find displeasing, we move to comfortable surroundings, even the most acutely lonely feel uncomfortable when they try to be too detached from what they know is unnatural and detrimental to their well-being.

Loneliness is a way of life, out of which it is quite difficult to fully depart. If the lonely do depart, they will leave behind a very significant part of their lives. Those who struggle to integrate become observers, perhaps on occasion raising their heads above the parapet to make a contribution to worldly affairs, but it is often too fleeting to make enough of an impression.

Humans are natural rebels and reluctant conformists. We can gauge this from our everyday behaviour and action. Being alone is a natural rebellion against social norms, perhaps inherited sometime when we were teenagers. Those teenagers who might find integrating into social groups a great struggle, may spend their lives alone and as fearful human vessels.

Sweet and Sour Dreams

A human, due to its very nature, dreams and plans. Just as we leave our conscious worlds at night to enter the vast unknown world of dreams, where we abandon logic and reason and enter worlds of absurdity and nonsense, we also spend our lives dreaming of what we want our lives to become.

Some people realise their dreams but through hard work and much personal sacrifice and personal loss. However, some dreams turn sour. Reality has a way of kicking us in the teeth.

Sour dreams we have to abandon. Perhaps there is a reason we have to taste sour dreams in life. Perhaps they lead us to the sweetest of all our dreams. We may have that one dream which stands way above all our other dreams.

Uncertainty Is Our Only Certainty

When we switch on the internet and television, we expect something to appear on the screen. When we wash, we expect to be cleansed. When we drink, we expect our thirst to be quenched.

What about life in general, where so much cannot be pre-determined? We do not know if we will be alive the next week, we can hope or presume, but we cannot be certain. It is uncertainty which pre-occupies our hearts and minds throughout our lives.

No one can predict so many forthcoming events. One is ignorant of the future, so little of life is certain, so much is uncertain or unpredictable.

Certain things are certain. But we have no way of knowing the times these things will occur. We can but wait. Death is one of these certainties. Only the time of when this will be is uncertain. We can chronicle our lives and reflect upon all the moments we faced uncertainties.

The Humble Speak the Universal Language

We all know of the shortness of time in life. We can try to think otherwise, that we can change the course of life and death, but we realise, if there was no death, there would be no life.

In this life, we communicate through human languages. One of them, depending on which ones we know. Language was created for the purpose of communication.

Only the humble speak the universal language created by God Almighty. When the human heart and soul are so obedient, they are honoured and blessed with the language of the spirit, which transcends all human languages. It is the language of peace and ultimate spiritual wisdom, transcending all human pettiness.

The humble do not crave or desire worldly pleasures and gratifications. They see life, not the world.

Limitations and Potentials

Life is an ever-changing and advancing process. We learn new things every day of our lives. Old knowledge is replaced, new knowledge becomes old. One thing we all learn is that we are limited. We will be unable to fulfil all of our desires, and at some stage of life, we are crushed by life. Some will not recover, others will turn their tragedy into fortune. Perhaps the human species needs to be taught an invaluable lesson, we are limited and subject to so many things outside our understanding and control. When we accept that we were created, we can better deal with pain and misfortune.

When we accept our limitations do we discover latent talents and potential alike. What is visible, what is latent takes a long time to manifest for us to realise we had it in ourselves all along. Sometimes and in some way being limited is also a strength, as it allows us to look within ourselves to bring out so much latent talent and potential. Until we see the very extent of our weaknesses, we will not see the very extent of our strengths.

Can We Exist Without Technology?

One thing that the 21st century has become synonymous with is technology. Technology is nothing new, it has been developing over a very considerable period, but what makes technology so special to us is that just about every aspect of life has been affected by it. Everything we do has some technological link or connection. Over a long period, technology has been shaping our lives. Now technology is so personal and intimate, it has become an artificial limb.

The question we need to pose is, can we live without technology? All we need do is look at our daily lives a minute at a time and see how technology personally affects us. We often overlook the technology in use.

We switch on the television or internet and subconsciously switch off the real world. The real world feels detached. Have we become subservient, perhaps submitting to our technology? Is technology enhancing our life or doing the opposite?

The Connection Between Our Brain and Mouth

The brain all of us know of, how powerful it is and what it can achieve. The brain is perpetually working, even when we disregard its functions. In most people's cases, another aspect of ours is the mouth.

Some people have more control over how much the mouth is used. Some are forever speaking and spewing out inanities and absurdities, others use it more sparingly, opting instead to use the mouth only when it is considered appropriate, speaking something after thinking on a particular subject.

The internal processes from the brain to the mouth are often not within human control. All of which that departs the mouth has undergone much conscious and subconscious activity.

Sometimes we utter something which belies our real intentions and meaning. Some people take much care, especially in public, to say what is deemed appropriate; others simply say what comes in their mouth.

Love is a Wonderful Feeling

We can imagine what it must feel like to float in the sky. There is such a great gulf between the sky and all of us down on earth, we can only look up in wonder at the sheer magnitude and brilliance of the sky.

What would it be like, if we could float in the clouds? Perhaps like it does to be in love when our emotions or feelings take over, even for a short time. Love is the greatest driver of our emotional lives; it makes us feel so good, there are simply no words to express how we feel.

Love is the greatest bond between ourselves and the Lord. Perhaps love is the greatest bond which can exist between two people. It transcends all of our petty concerns and obsessions.

Love is invisible yet it is everywhere we may care to look, we just do not see it. It is as real as anything visible and tangible on earth.

Love changes our dreams, our priorities for such a wonderful creation. It is from the lord, we are at the mercy of love. A cold heart will find it immensely difficult to feel love. When we can cry and laugh at the drop of a coin do we become aware that love has penetrated our hearts. No one can hold out against love for long.

Plus and Minus

Every life has its death or end. We all come to realise that earthly life is not eternal. It is always a painful lesson; every plus has its minus. Every joy has its sorrow. There is a minus to every plus and conversely a plus to every minus. Just as we take away from and in life, we also add to it or compound it. There must be a constant equilibrium in order for life to be harmonious. For every thing we lose or give up in life, there will in time be a compensation, whether these compensations adequately and satisfactorily substitute or make up for the losses, only time will tell. Certain losses cannot be financially compensated, for it is the minus that adds to the plus when we gain the loss, it will have enriched it in ways we can only but imagine, yet not comprehend.

Words and Music

We all communicate, even when we have nothing to say, our mere silence is communicating far more then we realise. Sometimes we do not need words to say what is inside us.

Music is a very potent and universal means of communication. There is a rhythm and harmony in music. Like silence, music too does not require words or language to convey feelings and thoughts. Communication is meant to be an exchange of information, whatever shape or form the communication takes. Music stirs up feelings and helps to jog memories.

Sometimes, words and music mingle to form songs. Songs draw both music and words to give it the complete shape. Music can be misread and misheard when words are joined to music. The song expresses feelings the musician wishes to convey, the words have to be right for the music.

Songs have to stir feelings.

Songs and music stir dormant feelings and re-ignite them; Love is the strongest of all feelings.

What Is Important?

What is important in life? It often takes a long time of exploration and disappointment before we know or realise what is important. As we pass through different stages of life does our view of the world and life change. It does take a long time before we come to the point of realisation and cognition of what is and what is not important in our lives and to us.

To each one, importance in the world and life is different; what for one may be important may not be for another.

In our youth, only what we want and our pleasures are important. In youth, the peripheral in our lives are different things.

One day, we realise that worldly life is transient and consequently of little or no real importance. As we grow older and advance in age, the world becomes less and less important.

Prevalence of the Materialistic

Mankind has been on Planet Earth for a considerable period of time, yet for some reason, we have not evolved in so many ways. We get embroiled in so many squabbles, proving the danger of being wholly materialistic, we get caught up in superficial and permanently trivial pursuits.

The worldly life has become concerned with petty matters and affairs. Materialism has seemed to have crept into every facet of our lives. Things of the worldly and materialistic steer us inevitably in the direction of the petty and the ultimately meaningless. Materialism shows its face in so many areas of modern or contemporary life.

The prevalence of the materialistic concerns the affairs of the self and how at the expense of others the self can progress. The materialistic are deluded if they think such a life is the key to happiness and prosperity.

Knowledge

How does one define knowledge? Do we simply define it as something which we know? Perhaps in its simplest form, it is that which we by chance know because the information crossed our paths? Each one shall have a different definition and interpretation. Which is valid would depend upon whether we wish for a relative or absolute conclusion. I suppose all information acquired by any of the senses is knowledge, be it through the eyes, ears or others. Would it be valid to suppose that information received would somehow be converted into knowledge?

Humankind has been obtaining knowledge for many centuries. Knowledge procurement was slower before television and the internet but somehow, it was gathered. Information in the contemporary world is of the essence for so many reasons, it takes less to no time for knowledge to travel the world.

Is there any such thing as absolute knowledge? Much of what we consider knowledge depends upon each individual. Knowledge can be broken down into so many trillions of components and linked to so many more trillions of components. We can link knowledge in one field to knowledge in so many others. Knowledge has trillions and trillions of branches, how we acquire our knowledge is sometimes a personal choice.

Technology has done much to change and determine how we acquire knowledge, whereas before, books were prevalent. For our knowledge procurement, now to a great extent, technology serves this role.

Damage or Injury is Not Always Visible

It is completely mind-blowing to consider how many civilisations have perished and disappeared off the face of the earth. What we are left with in the 21st century is human remnants, evolving and developing over many years.

All those buildings, schools, hospitals, universities form another era have been destroyed forever. All we have to remind ourselves of ancient civilisation is still buildings, colosseums, open-air theatres in Rome, Athens; Babylon; etc.

Damage or destruction to people, property, idea, etc., is not always visible, sometimes there is damage which is not instantly apparent. Often it requires far more time for our eyes to really open to injury and damage which lies beneath the surface. It is ever so easy to overlook so much in our lives today, where people rush around like headless chickens, just so that they can show that they have done something to show.

People who undergo psychological damage may have to, not out of choice, keep these injuries hidden. Either because of the pain or because of lack of sympathetic listeners. Just as with all the civilisations which have perished, it is without all the facts and details difficult to appreciate the scale of the injury. Trying to understand people who have to live with psychological damage for the rest of their lives is often far more difficult than we may have previously or originally thought.

Being Human Is More Than a Genetic Reality

We go hither and thither in our multifarious pursuits. How much we happen to achieve and accomplish is hard to say. We will have many disappointments and failures. On the other hand, we will have our fair share of joy and successes.

Regardless of our outward ambitions, we sometimes become oblivious of our true lifelong predicament, i.e., that we are human and a part of humanity. We can, and often do, become proud and too ambitious for our own good. We can allow our aspirations to supersede our needs to look after our fellows. Unfortunately, courtesy and good manners seem things of the past.

Being human is more than a familial and genetic reality. As a member of a particular family, we are not secluded from the rest of humanity. We must never regard our existence and life as our absolute right. Life is a privilege and should be treated with this regard and respect. What have we, of our own, done to deserve a life?

When we look within do we find a clearer answer for why we are alive. There is, regardless of all superficial differences and barriers, a common and consistent theme running throughout human life, i.e., a regard for the Divine and all life created by Him. We deny this knowledge at our peril. Our genetic story may be unique to us, but what story will our humanity convey to others?

The Brain's Vast Information Storage

Everything we see, hear, smell, taste and touch will somehow or other reach a certain area of the brain. Where these happen to be, neurologists could state. All the same, even to a lay person, the sheer power and scale of information stored by the brain would be enough to have anyone's head spinning around for a considerable time.

It is perhaps because we are ordinarily oblivious of the actual scale or amount of work carried out by the brain that we are able to undertake our chores. If we were always cognisant of the sheer magnitude of works performed by our brain, we would freeze in contemplation.

The brain is, however we consider it, a marvel to behold. What from all of the books that we read, to the conversations we have, the amount of information permeating our brains appears unlimited. All of this information, perhaps not always in use, remains in store for a very long time indeed. Otherwise, this information, when not in use, languishes in the brain.

The brain would make the strongest computer seem very pedestrian indeed. No matter how powerful a computer appears, it pales into insignificance when the true and real immensity of the brain is considered. The computer, at its best and most powerful, probably only corresponds with a single brain cell.

Machines Should Never Be Considered in the Absolute

It is undoubtedly the case that in the first part of the 21st century, we have become surrounded by machines. From the cars we drive, to the televisions we watch, we are subconsciously adjusted to a machine-dominated world. If we take this a stage further, we may find a lot of clues to what we once were.

Machines, no matter how efficient and helpful, should never be regarded as being the ultimate and absolute. They merely supplement our lives and not to determine our thoughts and feelings. Alas, for some, the machines do really determine and dictate their fashions. For them, it is necessary to accept machines as a relevant part of life.

Let us consider the computer for a moment. What some twenty years before was still something unobtainable and vastly primitive, has been transformed into a compact tool of convenience. It is capable of more than storage and retrieval. It can compute, analyse, compare, etc. Nonetheless, we may, and sometimes do, become fascinated by the powers and strengths inbuilt to the computer. Switched off, it will serve no purpose.

Machines, whether we consider cars, radios or television, should not prevent us from enjoying our real and invaluable joys and gifts of imagination and creative thought. It is so simple to switch on the television set or computer and permit our imaginative powers to languish. Many have, for whatever reason, become akin to zombies and robots, incapable of rising to the challenge of creative thinking.

If a link can be found between our minds and our lifestyles and the amount of automation in our lives, we may come to regret having become so deluded and obsessed by machines. We are, whether we think our lives have been enhanced by the machines and automation, inextricably linked to the machine culture.

Like a Good Book, Life Comes to an End

What a wonderful experience it seems at the time to embark on a voyage or journey. Commencing a book is very much like a start of a voyage, of which we are at the time ignorant. Unlike viewing films, for which we never attain 100% concentration, reading a book can only be enjoyed with absolute and undivided attention. The moment that we sense ourselves slipping away into other thoughts, we subsequently lose track.

Like a book, life, to an extent, can be regarded as an interesting and fascinating experience or journey. Just as we start to read a book, so each new day begins. What actually happens, may for us be incidental and out of our control. No one has the day entirely as they might hope.

As we progress and digress in life, our time may seem eternal, never to come to an end. But if we compare life to a book, we will realise that like a book, life too will, at some time, come to an end. We will experience all forms of surprises and the unexpected, perhaps elevating us above our rather-mediocre lifestyles. Books always have far more contained between the covers than we may have otherwise thought. Unlike a book, life is intangible and invisible. It is an experience which cannot be written like an essay or book.

Public Face – Private Make-Up

Whenever we set foot out of our abodes, we need to transform our manners and demeanour so as to influence those whom we meet or hope to meet. Many people are exceptional public speakers and performers. Others may be immensely impressed and awe-struck. We can proffer a certain persona and character traits. Our manner may be so natural. Anything at which we work at perfecting, may to the untrained ears and eyes, as well as to the assuming, appear natural. The point is, when we are outside of our homes, we need to convince and, to some extent, make believe.

Before we leave our homes, we place some make-up not only on our faces, but also on our behaviour, speech, state of mind, body language and facial expressions. Many people who do exactly this may be surprised at how extensively they put on this make-up. It may be done subconsciously, seeming to be second-nature.

We can imagine ourselves as subconscious actors, with our own roles and lines, yet to many, this comes so naturally, they may not even always be cognisant that life can be one big show. An illustration of this is a job interview. We know that if we really want the job, we will have to put on a very good and impressive show.

In life's epilogue do we see the person as he or she really is. When there are no lines to be said and costumes to be put on do we see the real us.

The World Will Always Overwhelm Us

The world, as we love, loathe, know, ignore and comprehend, will always be too overwhelming for us. For human comprehension and perception, it is too vast and mysterious. We inhabit and change the world, yet any thoughts we have of comprehending it should be removed.

As we are aware, the world is not merely and solely what we think it to be. There are so many other characteristics which will baffle us; after all, we are dealing not only with the physical world.

Whether we consider the world from an historical perspective, we are dealing with trillions of events of which we have no cognition and understanding. Only when we take an ardent look at history do we discover so much more than we may have otherwise thought.

With increasing technology, more and more information is becoming available. The easier it is becoming to search and research, the more we realise how ignorant we truly are. Even with new and ever-advancing technologies, we come to the understanding that the world indeed is very overwhelming.

What Does It Mean to Be a Human Being?

"Being human means being tuned into life.
Sometimes experiencing happiness, sometimes experiencing strife."

The above verses are taken from a poem titled 'What Does It Mean to Be a Human Being?'. Just as this question is so straightforward to answer, it is also very difficult to answer. If we consider ourselves from one viewpoint, we may find supplying an answer so very easy. But when we consider the question with a bit more depth, we realise that such a straightforward and quick, and perhaps hastily derived notion, does not suffice. Consider this thought for a moment. The human being is a confused and complex life-force. Being unsure and ignorant of life is all part of the course. We need to take many issues into account. Supposedly, everyone will come up with a unique and different definition. When we look at ourselves at some length, we will find certain unique qualities, this enabling us to take a pause from our present endeavours and seriously consider and ponder on what a human being is. As we discover, there are so many facets to the human being, some obvious and others not so obvious. When we are deeply touched and affected, our views and perspectives undergo a change. Each one knows that as we have so many unique qualities, we are essentially very much the same.

A human being is a collection of many different gardens. Each garden will have its rows of thorn bushes, as well as its assortment of roses. The thorns which comprise our experiences and disappointments will cause us enormous anguish and pain. The roses, on the other hand, will allay some of this pain. What we see in ourselves, we also see in others. A human being is a multi-dimensional personality which has been shaped and re-shaped over many years. Our perceptions do change and transform us throughout our lives.

Understanding what the human being is, as we discover, a more difficult and considerable quest. In order to understand ourselves as human beings as separate from other lifeforms, it is necessary to take many complex and intricate factors into account. We need to see our past and our present, always accepting that what distinguishes our past from our present is change.

What Does It Mean to Be a Human Being?
(2)

Of the human being, some of us will offer very clear and concise definitions, yet others will provide very ambiguous and lengthy definitions. We are, to some extent, masters of our own lives. The human being is a marriage of his or her potentials and aspirations, as well as his or her limitations and disabilities. Where in one regard, we are free, another will be restricted. Conversely, where we are restrained, another may be free. While a part of us is asleep, another is awake. While our conscious is asleep, our subconscious is awake, e.g., our dream states. While our conscious is awake, our subconscious is asleep. So holds true throughout life. As one part sleeps, another is awake.

We realise that we are many different things at different times of our lives. One moment, we are a philosopher, another a pupil, another a parent, another a child, another an athlete, another a counsellor. Each occasion brings out a different human facet in us.

As human beings, we hold so much within. We may not always reveal what we do hold. There could be any number of reasons for this. Sometimes we do not know what we do know. What languishes within the subconscious is very hard to answer. Who knows how many trillions of memories and thoughts reside within the subconscious? The subconscious is such a mystery to us. It is a great task to put all into one unit. As we find, a collection is analysed by the subconscious. If we could unravel and fathom all the information contained within our hearts and minds, this information would so easily wrap the earth at least a hundred fold. We are neither a whole as a package, nor are we individual units. The human being is a part of something much more superior to us.

A Wise Counsel

No one can survive or go through life on one's own. There comes a time in everyone's life when events take a turn for worse. When the whole world seems against us, we need a counsel who can advise and pull us through. Not everyone's advice is helpful or useful. Many people, contrary to appearance, have nothing to contribute. But in the event of our finding someone whose advice is helpful, we should, in our better judgement, hold on to and embrace that person as tightly as possible.

Some people have great insight and prove very good counsels. To them, all situations are unproblematic. They have a way of seeing and observing life and tackling any difficulty with their usual calm. Their advice, as well as approach to life, seems so markedly different from those who take a pessimistic look and analysis of life.

Failing a wise counsel, if one prays each and every day, one shall receive the help of the wisest counsel of all. God, our Lord, is with us forever, both in our happy times and in our not so happy times. All wisdom and knowledge originates from God, which is then merely dispersed throughout his universe, of which we incorporate a certain amount. If one listens closely to wise words, one will agree or consent that these words are not man-made but of a much higher status and level.

No matter what the situation or condition might be, the wise counsel always has something very great to expound. In its essence, wisdom transcends all our difficulties and anxieties. Wisdom is a conglomeration of all that is different and all that is similar in humans.

Life Breeds Life

Life is a topic, unlike anything fleeting or worldly, about which we can discourse for a long time but never tire. Life is like an elastic which stretches for eternity. If we take a normal elastic band, it will stretch only so far. But the same does not apply to life.

Life breeds life. The living breeds the living. If we consider the trillions of varieties of life, we come to realise the infinite possibilities of which we may ordinarily not be aware. The food we eat, the drink we consume, the books we read, the music which we listen to are all a part and parcel of life.

One generation perpetuates life for another. What the former generation does today, or has done in the past, will affect the lives of many people in the future.

When we attend a live event, a concert or a play, there is a profusion of life and change in our otherwise-dormant feelings and desire. In this rather-robotic and seemingly sophisticated lifestyle of so very many have we become conditioned. At times in our daily travels, we might feel scared and really embarrassed to demonstrate our feelings. When we attend a concert do these inhibitions become forgotten, if only for a short time.

What gives meaning to our lives is the utilisation of our natural talents. If we are more content to accept the pervading superficial lifestyles, we may permit our talents no scope for experimentation and development. Life is far more complex and unpredictable than we may ordinarily think. If we take perhaps the most important ingredient of life, i.e., love, we will subsequently discover that love breeds its like. If we display or demonstrate affection towards another, love may be reciprocated, or else dispersed to new and wider pastures.

Everyone Wants to Change Something

Everything has a part to play in the world. There are so many things that we are not always aware of. It is the same with people. We often overlook so many people in our travels which perhaps not until later that we see or notice.

There is always a certain something we wish to change. There is always some aspect of our lives or the world which we desperately wish to change. This may be a far-off possibility. There may be reasons for why we can never quite offer our wholehearted support and commitment to this one cause. We may be too busy in our jobs, with our families, bringing up the kids, having so many priorities and engagements that the opportunity seems so elusive. As everyone discovers, life does not move in the way we might wish or hope.

Perhaps we want to change the ways in which people think, act, behave, pray. But for everything we want to alter, a great deal of stamina is required. It might even take years before there is a result.

If we were content in our states, there would never be a need to change. Neither in our complacent states would we try to change the world, nor would we try to change ourselves. We would sink deeper into our states of complacency and satisfaction.

Human Spirit

Life is so short. One moment, we are laughing and chatting away, without a care in the world. Before we know it, all this is over. For as long as we are alive, the spiritual realm is beyond our sight and comprehension. Perhaps it is more common for us to try to justify everything in the physical terms and sense. We can forget that the physical which we think we know ever so well is merely a mirage of something which we do not understand. Nothing in life is permanent. Just as we hold on to someone or something, they or we have to leave. Only our contributions to the world live on, while we ourselves depart for good.

As we are so bound by the physical, ultimately the short-term, we are also ignorant of the true nature of the spiritual. In some, the feeling of spirituality cannot be explained in words. It goes beyond language and emotions. Spirituality, unlike physical life, is perfect in structure and is in complete harmony with the Almighty God.

Those not fortunate enough to experience this divine feeling will continue to judge life in terms of what they can see and hear. They may remain unconvinced that life's true and real purpose is not to indulge always in secular matters, but to strive for spiritual enlightenment and purity.

Once we enter God's holy light, we come to realise that the world we might take so much for granted is a mere transient trap which can engulf the unbelieving. The great question is: do we reside in the dark or do we try to approach the greatest light of them all.

Life's Unique Language

Whomever we may or may not be, and wherever we may happen to live, is inconsequential as far as the aspect of life is concerned. These facts or realities are short-lasting. Who we are or may be is really out of our control. We are what we are, not out of anything which we have done. Each and every individual has some family or heritage and spiritual life. We may try to demean or dismiss various aspects of our lives, but irrespective of our thoughts, they cannot be rubbed away like a teacher removes something he or she may have written on the blackboard. The chalk paints everything else we have achieved to date in our lives.

Life's language, unlike man-made languages, is universal. It has been written and constructed by God Almighty. We are all users and practitioners of this language, greatest of them all. Life's language is comprehensible from the moment that we are born. It is simple and un-complex enough for us to obey and understand. The reality may, for some, be very different. Some people may try to construct their own grammar and sentences, and so flout the universal and unchanging rules of this life's language.

Unlike all the languages which we use today, e.g., English, German, Latin, Greek, etc., life's language has never changed, and never will it do so. It, like life itself, is constant. If and when we study and put life's language under the spotlight do we come to realise that it has not once changed.

The very fact that we have eyes and hair on our head, or not as the case might be, and a distinctive personality and character and temperament means that we are, whether we like it or not, bound to life's language, in all aspects of conscious and subconscious life, we are somehow making use of life's unique language.

An Electronic Universe in a Social World

The past thirty years or so have seen or witnessed a technological revolution of the magnitude or character no one had probably envisaged or foreseen. First there was the transistor, followed by the colour television set, followed by the cassette recorder, followed by the Wi-Fi, followed by the compact disc, followed by the laser disc. The hardware has decreased in size while the capacity to store information has increased many times.

Our social world seems to have decreased in size, or grown smaller, while the electronic world seems to have grown into a universe. All we need to do is consider the influence of our computers, television sets, mobile phones, Walkmans and all the other gadgets to realise how reliant we have become on electronic goods. There is a general tendency to switch our television sets on and sit back while the purveyors of information feed whatever they want us to swallow.

It does not seem to bother many that they may not receive the social interaction that previous generations took so much for granted. The thrill of seeing and meeting people has dissipated somewhat.

Without wishing to appear alarmist, the internet is further eroding what little genuine social communication there remains.